KEEPING HEALTHY
Safety

Text by Carol Ballard
Photography by Robert Pickett

HODDER
Wayland

an imprint of Hodder Children's Books

TITLES IN THE KEEPING HEALTHY SERIES:

• Personal Hygiene • Eating • Safety
• Exercise • Relationships • Harmful Substances

For more information on this series and other Hodder Wayland titles, go to www.hodderwayland.co.uk

© 2004 White-Thomson Publishing Ltd
Produced by White-Thomson Publishing Ltd
2/3 St Andrew's Place, Lewes, BN7 1UP

Editor:	Elaine Fuoco-Lang
Consultant:	Chris Sculthorpe, East Sussex, Brighton & Hove Healthy School Scheme Co-ordinator
Inside design:	Joelle Wheelwright
Cover design:	Hodder Wayland
Photographs:	Robert Pickett
Proofreader:	Jane Colgan
Artwork:	Peter Bull

Published in Great Britain in 2004 by Hodder Wayland, an imprint of Hodder Children's Books. Reprinted in 2004
Hodder Children's Books, a division of Hodder Headline Limited, 338 Euston Road, London, NW1 3BH.

The right of Carol Ballard to be identified as the author of this Work has been asserted by her in accordance with the Copyright, Designs and Patents Act 1988.

British Library Cataloguing in Publication Data
Ballard, Carol
   Safety. - (Keeping Healthy)
   1. Accidents - Prevetion - Juvenile literature
   2. Risk assessment - Juvenile literature
   I. Title
   613.6

ISBN 0 7502 4338 4

Printing and binding at C&C China.

Acknowledgements:

The publishers would like to thank the following for their assistance with this book: the staff and children at Drapers Mills Primary School, Margate, Kent.

Picture acknowledgements:
Tim Pannell/Corbis 5 bottom, Yang Liu/Corbis 6, Mug Shots/Corbis 10, Ronnie Kaufman/Corbis 11 top, Progressive Image/Corbis 12 bottom, Daniel Mirer/Corbis 17 bottom, George Hall/Corbis 23 bottom, Firefly Productions/Corbis 24, Corbis 25, David Butow/Corbis SABA 29 right; Angela Hampton 14, 16, 19 top, 21; Hodder Wayland Picture Library 8, 9 top, 11 bottom; Robert Pickett 9 bottom, 12 top, 13, 15, 17 top, 18, 19 bottom, 20, 23 top, 26, 27, 28, 29 left; WTPix 4, 22.

The photographs in this book are of models who have granted their permission for their use in this title.

Contents

Safety matters

Wherever you are, whatever you are doing, it is important to be safe. Adults, like your parents and teachers, can help you to be safe but they cannot do everything. You have a big role to play too. If you know what it is safe to do, where it is safe to go and who it is safe to be with, you can avoid a lot of accidents. Using your knowledge about safety can help to keep you safe, as well as other people around you.

▼ *Being safe when playing sport is important. Wearing protective clothing can help to prevent you from getting injured.*

4

This book tells you about some of the ways in which you can stay safe at home and when you go out to play. It gives you some suggestions for keeping safe on the roads and other places such as swimming pools and beaches. You'll find guidance about first aid for yourself and other people and advice about what to do in an emergency.

▲ *Signs like this are warnings about dangers around you.*

So, why not do something about being responsible for your own safety? Make sure you always listen to and follow advice from adults you can trust, such as parents and teachers.

► *Take care when out playing with your friends.*

At home

We all like to think of our homes as being safe places, but accidents can happen all too easily. Many accidents are the result of people being careless or lazy.

Kitchens contain many things that, if not used properly, could be dangerous. Sharp knives, cookers, boiling water and cleaning materials all need to be used very carefully.

Many of the things we use every day need electricity. An adult will probably have checked that all the wires and connections are safe, but if you spot an old, frayed wire make sure you tell somebody. Follow these safety rules:

● Never touch anything electrical, especially with wet hands.

● Never poke a socket or appliance with anything.

● Never take anything electrical to pieces.

● Always switch electrical appliances OFF when they are not being used.

▲ *Microwave ovens, toasters and cookers can all be dangerous if they are not used correctly.*

Being untidy is the cause of many accidents! People can easily trip over toys and other things that are left lying around, so make sure you put things away when you have finished with them.

It is a long way to fall from the top of the stairs to the bottom! It makes sense not to play on or around stairs or outdoor steps.

▲ *DANGER! This symbol shows us that we should take care.*

⩘ Action Zone

Toddlers and young children are particularly at risk from harmful substances like cleaning materials, as they are still exploring the world around them and do not know what is safe to eat and drink and what is not. Cleaning materials should always be kept in their original containers. Do not use them unless an adult has told you to, and always read the safety warnings on the label. You can help to keep younger brothers and sisters safe by keeping things like cleaning materials out of their reach, and putting them away properly. If the cupboard door has a child-proof catch, make sure it is fastened.

▲ *Household chemicals, such as bleach, may have these symbols on them. They are warning us that the product can be poisonous (left) and corrosive (right).*

Play safe!

Playing is good fun – and by being sensible you can make sure that your games are safe for you and the people you are playing with.

If you are playing with younger children, you need to think about their safety as well as your own. If your toys or games have small pieces, then save them for a time when young children are not around, as they often put little things in their mouths and can easily choke. Remember they are smaller than you so try not to play boisterous games in which they might fall over or get hurt.

Toys and games

Toys and games that need batteries should be looked after carefully. When the battery runs down, ask an adult to help you change it. If a battery has leaked, ask an adult to make the toy safe.

When you have finished playing with a toy or game, make sure you tidy up and put it away properly, so that nobody else will trip over it. This is good for everybody else in your house – and it is good for your game too!

▲ *Fairgrounds are a great place to have fun, but if you are with young children make sure you take extra care of them.*

Where to play

Try to choose a sensible place to play. A garden is a good place for a running around game, but a landing or staircase is not as you could easily fall downstairs. If you want to go to a park or playground, always ask an adult first, and make sure you tell them where you are going, who you will be with and when you will be back. Once you've done that, make sure you stick to what you have said – don't get tempted to go somewhere else instead.

◄ *Playing outside is fun but make sure an adult knows where you are.*

✓ Action Zone

Are all your toys safe to play with? Go and check your toy cupboard. Take each toy and game out one at a time and look carefully at it. Is it broken? Does it have any sharp edges? Could it hurt you or a younger child in any way? If the answer to any of these is 'YES', tell an adult so they can make it safe.

▶ *Broken toys can be very dangerous. Make sure you let an adult know if one of your toys is broken. Here you can see a broken windscreen on this car has left sharp edges which should only be handled by an adult.*

Out and about . . .

It is fun to go out to play or to be with your friends. Think about how you can keep yourself safe.

Some places are safer than others. Unless you are with an adult, avoid playing in woods and sheltered spots – open parks and playgrounds are much better as there are people all around. Try not to play near water as there is always a danger of falling in. Frozen ponds and streams are great to look at, but never be tempted to try to walk on them as the ice is often much thinner than you expect and can easily break under your weight.

▲ When you are out playing remember the importance of safety.

Out on your own

It is a good idea to stay with at least one other person rather than going off on your own, as you can help each other if there is a problem. Although it makes sense never to talk to strangers, if you get separated from the people you set off with, you might need some help. In a store or shopping centre, there will usually be an official person around for you to talk to. If not, look out for an adult out with their own family and explain your problem to them – they will probably be able to help you.

▲ *If you are out in cold weather, wearing layers and warm clothing is a very sensible option.*

Clothing

Wherever you are going, make sure you are wearing the right clothing. If it is a cold day, wrap up well. Several layers of clothes will keep you warmer than one thick layer. A waterproof layer is a good idea too, just in case it starts to rain. If you are going to be out when it gets dark, make sure you can be seen by motorists and other people. Reflective strips on your clothes show up in bright car headlights and help to make you stand out in the dark. Carrying a torch is also a good idea, so you can see and be seen.

 # Healthy Hints

Feet are important – and so are the things that you wear on them! We all like to wear fashionable trainers and other shoes, but just being fashionable does not make them the best footwear for every activity. Think carefully about what you are going to be doing and choose footwear that matches the activity – for example, strong boots are good for walking over rough ground, trainers with grippy soles are good for playing on climbing frames and waterproof wellies are good for splashing around in puddles.

▲ *Footwear is very important and isn't just a fashion statement. Protecting yourself from falling over is far more important.*

On the pavement

Walking on the pavement or footpath is usually safe – but do you know how to cross a road safely?

First, find a safe place to cross. If there is a pedestrian crossing nearby, make sure you use it. If not, find a place where the road is straight and you can see clearly in both directions. Stand at the edge of the pavement. Look first in the direction the traffic is coming from on your side of the road – usually to your right. If there is nothing, look the other way – usually to your left. If there is nothing coming, look in the first direction again. If that is still clear, walk quickly and sensibly across the road.

▲ **Make sure you are careful when crossing the road.**

If you use a pedestrian crossing with lights, press the button and wait for the signal that tells you it is safe to cross. At many crossings, an illuminated man on the sign changes from red to green when you can cross safely. At other crossings, it may say 'Walk' or something similar.

◀ **In the US, road marshalls help children to cross the road to their school.**

Never be tempted to cross a road from behind a vehicle such as an ice cream van. You will be hidden by the vehicle and so a car driver may not see you until it is too late, and then you could be badly hurt.

Playing ball on a pavement or on a road is dangerous. If you do play on a pavement, never run into the road to get your ball back. You could easily be hit by a car or other vehicle.

▶ *Playing with a ball is fine, but make sure you find somewhere safe to play.*

On the road

Many people are killed or seriously injured on the roads every day, so it is important to be as sensible as you can and take all possible safety precautions.

Motor vehicles

Cars, buses and coaches can be dangerous for the passengers. Always put your seat belt on, and do not stand up or move around the vehicle while it is moving. Never distract the driver – he or she needs to concentrate on their driving.

Riding a bicycle is a good way to get around, but before you go out onto a road, make sure you can ride your bike confidently and safely. Make sure you know what the common road signs mean and that you know how to signal when you are turning right or left. Remember to stop and look both ways before you ride out into the road, just as you would if you were going to cross a road on foot.

▶ *Wearing a seatbelt is the law and it helps protect you and the person in front of you if you have an accident.*

Bicycles

Ride on the correct side of the road and obey all road signs and traffic signals. Check behind before you turn or change lanes. If you are cycling with other people, do not ride more than two side by side, and on narrow or busy roads always ride one behind the other. Remember it is dangerous to hold onto another cyclist or carry a passenger on your bike.

▶ *Wearing a helmet and reflective clothing is very important when riding your bike.*

 # Healthy Hints

Follow these guidelines to make sure your bike is safe to ride:

● Make sure your bike is the right size for you – without bending your legs, you should be able to put both feet on the ground when sitting on the saddle.

● Check the brakes work properly and the tyres are pumped up. The chain should be oiled and adjusted properly.

● Use a bike bag or panniers to carry things – putting a bag on the handlebars makes it hard to keep your balance, and it could get caught in the front wheel.

● Wear a cycle helmet and reflective and fluorescent clothing.

● If you will be out in the dark, make sure your front and back lights are working properly.

▲ *It is important to keep your bike safe as well as yourself. Make sure your tyres are always fully pumped.*

At the pool

Swimming pools are great places to have fun! But having fun does not mean forgetting how to stay safe.

Do not swim unless there is an adult watching. Most swimming pools have an adult on duty, often sitting on a raised platform so they can see everything that is happening. If you have a problem, try to attract their attention by shouting or waving your arms.

Unless you are a strong swimmer, stay in the shallow end of the pool. Check you can stand up – if you cannot put your feet on the bottom of the pool, go back to shallower water. Usually the depth is marked on the wall of the pool so you can check how deep the water is where you are.

▲ *If you aren't a very experienced swimmer make sure an adult is with you, or watching you.*

▲ *When you are learning to swim, a float helps you to gain confidence in the water.*

Think about other pool users. Try not to splash other people, and never try to hold somebody under the water. If you want to dive in, go to the deep end of the pool. If you want to jump in, make sure nobody else is in the area. Obey the rules of the pool and only use balls, floats and other equipment when and where it is allowed.

The area around the pool is often wet and slippery so always walk around rather than running.

 # Healthy Hints

One of the good things about swimming in a swimming pool is that the water is clean and safe. All the time, the water in the pool is being changed. Before clean water flows into the pool, chemicals are added to kill any germs. A constant stream of dirty water flows out of the pool. You can play your part in keeping the pool clean for yourself and other swimmers to enjoy. Remember to go to the toilet before you swim. Avoid wearing outdoor shoes when you are in the pool surroundings and, if there is a footbath, make sure you use it. Never drop rubbish into or around the pool.

▲ *The lifeguard under the umbrella is ensuring the children are safe.*

At the beach

Many people have wonderful holidays at the beach – but beaches can be dangerous unless you follow a few simple guidelines.

Always check the beach is safe for swimming, and do not go into the water without permission. On flat beaches you imagine the sand going on forever under the water, but they can suddenly dip down and the water can quickly get much deeper than you expect.

▶ *Inflatables are great fun, but should be used with care when at the beach.*

Strong currents can be dangerous too, as you can get pulled away from the beach. Many beaches have special safety flags showing areas where it is safe to swim and other areas where it is more dangerous. Look for the flags and stay within the safe areas. Inflatables are great fun but should not be used on the sea as they can get swept out into deep water by the waves and current.

◀ *Rock pools are home to different animals, but make sure that you are careful as even shallow water can be dangerous.*

Cliffs and caves

It can be tempting to explore cliffs and caves, but there may be hidden dangers. Do not climb cliffs unless an adult is with you as you may fall. Do not go into caves alone, and make sure you never wander round a cliff head into the next bay as you may get cut off when the tide rushes in. Before you play around at the foot of cliffs, check there is not a sign warning of falling rocks.

Rocks on beaches are good for clambering over, but remember that seaweed and water can make them very slippery, so be careful where you put your feet. Walk carefully and don't run.

▲ *The beach can be inviting but be aware of the dangers.*

Action Zone

Nobody likes to play or sunbathe on a dirty beach. Try to make sure that you leave the beach as clean and tidy as you can. Put all your litter in a bin if there is one, or take it home with you. Tins and cans may have sharp edges that can cause a nasty cut. Glass is dangerous too as it can easily be broken.

▲ *Try to avoid taking tins and glass onto the beach. Choose things to eat and drink that come in plastic containers instead.*

Computers and communications

Computers and mobile phones make communications easy – but there are some risks that you should be aware of and avoid.

Mobile phones

Mobile phones are a great way to stay in touch with your friends and family, but some scientists now think that using a mobile for long periods may lead to health problems. A hands-free set may help to reduce this risk, as you do not need to hold the phone to your head when you use it.

▶ **Using a mobile phone for long periods is not a good idea.**

Computers

Many families have computers and are connected to the Internet. Some people think it is better to have the computer in a room that the whole family uses, rather than in a bedroom, so that other people might spot a problem you have not noticed. It's friendlier too, as you're not shutting yourself away from the rest of the family.

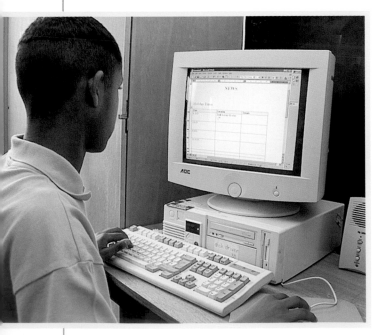

◀ **Computers are great for communicating, but ensure you are aware of the dangers.**

Chat rooms

Chat rooms are fun, but you need to take care. Always tell an adult what you are doing, and perhaps who you are chatting with. Never ever give your home address, school address or telephone number to someone in a chat room, and never arrange to meet somebody you have met in a chat room. You have no way of checking up on them and they may be pretending to be someone very different from who they really are.

Sometimes you may feel upset or worried by something you find on the Internet, or by something that is said in a chat room or on the telephone. If this happens, tell an adult so they can sort it out for you and stop it happening again.

Games

Some people who play computer games a lot can actually become addicted to them. This can cause all sorts of problems, and can take a long time to get over. Try to limit the length of time you spend using your computer, and make sure you get plenty of active fun as well.

Healthy Hints

Your body was not designed to sit in one place for hours on end staring at a little screen! Be kind to your body – give it a break now and again by getting up and moving around a bit. Your eyes will get tired if they stare at the screen too much, so try not to use the computer for very long spells. Try to sit straight too, so that your back doesn't get stiff and bunched up.

▲ *Playing computer games is fine in moderation.*

Fire!

▲ *A US fire engine goes into action.*

We have all heard the wailing of fire engine sirens as they rush to tackle a blaze somewhere. Fires are dangerous and you should know some basic safety precautions.

One of the first signs of fire is usually smoke. A smoke alarm can detect smoke long before it is noticeable by people, and makes a loud noise so you know there is danger.

If you hear a smoke alarm going off, make your way sensibly out of the building.

Preventing fires

If a fire does start, do not try to put it out on your own. Get out of the building, call the fire brigade and do not go back into the building for any reason at all, however important it may seem to you.

You can help to prevent fires from starting by not playing with matches or cigarette lighters, not throwing things onto open fires and not playing near heaters.

It can be all too easy to start fires outdoors too. Matches are just as dangerous outside, especially in dry weather, as grass and other plants can easily catch fire and the flames may spread very quickly. Never try to light a bonfire outside without an adult to help you.

▲ *Candles, matches and lighters are not toys to be played with.*

ᚿᚾ Action Zone

It is very unlikely that there will ever be a fire at your home – but, just in case, it is important that you know exactly how you would get to safety. Draw a floor plan of your home, marking on stairs, hallways, doors and windows. Each room should have two different exit routes, in case one is blocked. Talk to the rest of your family and check that you all have your escape routes planned. Make sure you can get out of windows if necessary. Choose a safe place outside where all the family can meet once you've escaped from the building.

▲ *A fireman fights a blaze.*

Safe celebrations

Bonfires and fireworks are part of many celebrations and are great to watch. There are many public displays and these are carefully organised so that everything is as safe as possible. If you have fireworks at home, remember that they are dangerous so it is important to behave sensibly. Follow the Firework Code, and try to make sure that those around you do so too:

● All fireworks should be handled by an adult and not by children.

● Store fireworks in a metal box and only take out one at a time. Never put fireworks in a pocket.

● A torch should be used to read the instructions on each firework. The instructions should be followed carefully.

▲ *Fireworks are great fun to watch but you should never play with them.*

- Stand well away from fireworks as sparks can travel long distances.

- Never go back to a firework that has been lit.

- Never throw fireworks.

- Keep pets indoors and safe.

People often light candles at times of celebration. Candles should always stand on a heatproof base, well away from anything that could dangle into the flame. They should never be left alight in a room when nobody is there.

Christmas lights are very pretty too, but before they are plugged in an adult should always check that the wires are safe.

▶ *Kwanzaa candles are lit to celebrate the African/ American cultural holiday, first celebrated in 1966.*

¡?/ Fantastic Facts

Gunpowder was invented in China more than 1200 years ago, and this is also where the first fireworks were made. The colour of a firework depends on the type of metal it contains. Different metals burn with different colours. Strontium gives red sparks, copper gives blue sparks, boron gives green sparks and magnesium gives bright silvery-white sparks.

First aid

We all hurt ourselves from time to time. You can treat some minor injuries yourself, but more serious accidents will need to be treated by an adult and sometimes by a doctor or first aider. If you are in any doubt about what to do, always ask an adult for help.

To treat a small cut or graze, clean the skin thoroughly with water and antiseptic. Sometimes you may need to cover it with a plaster.

▶ *If you cut yourself it is important to carefully clean the area with an antiseptic wipe.*

▼ *A wasp should not sting you unless you annoy it.*

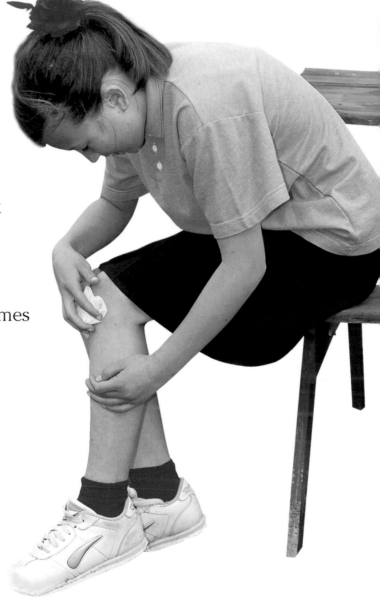

Insect stings and bites can hurt a lot! Some creams and sprays can take away the stinging feeling, but always check with an adult before you use them, to make sure you are doing the right thing.

If you fall and it hurts a lot to move, stay where you are and get a friend to go for help. If a friend falls and cannot move without a lot of pain, do not try to move them. Go and get help as quickly as you can.

A burn or scald needs immediate action to take the heat away from the skin. If you can, run cold water over the skin until it stops hurting quite so much. Never put anything on burnt skin, and always ask an adult for help as soon as you can.

◀ *If you are hurt, ask a friend for help.*

 # Healthy Hints

Your skin is your body's outer protective layer, preventing dirt and germs getting inside your body. When you cut yourself, your skin is broken, so it is easy for germs to get inside. It is important to clean a cut or graze thoroughly to prevent this happening. Washing with lots of water will flush any dirt away from the cut. An antiseptic wipe or spray will kill any germs that remain. Covering the cut with a plaster will help to keep it clean while the skin heals.

▲ *These plasters and creams are for use on minor cuts or grazes.*

27

Emergency!

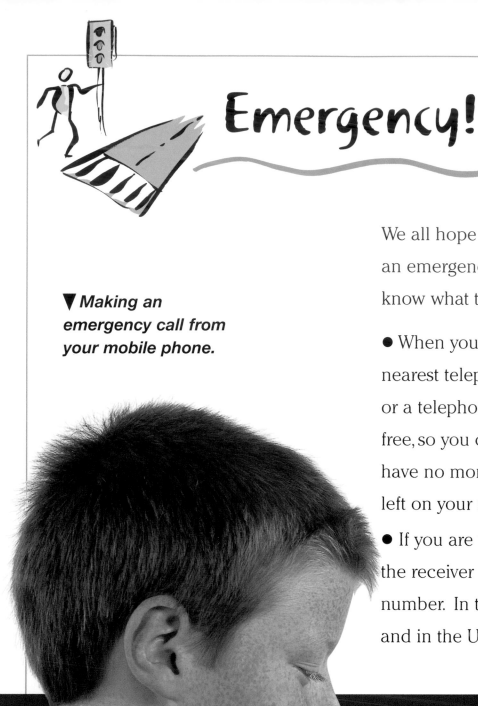

▼ *Making an emergency call from your mobile phone.*

We all hope we never have to deal with an emergency, but it is a good idea to know what to do, just in case.

● When you need help quickly, go to the nearest telephone. You can use a mobile or a telephone box. Emergency calls are free, so you can make one even if you have no money or if there is no money left on your mobile.

● If you are using a telephone box, lift the receiver and dial the emergency number. In the UK this is '999' and in the US it is '911'.

- When the operator answers, they will ask you which service you require. You need to tell them whether you need the police, fire brigade, ambulance, coastguard – or all of them.

- The operator will connect you to the emergency service you need. Stay as calm as you can. Listen to the questions the operator asks and answer them carefully. They will need to know where you are, what has happened and who is in trouble. Sometimes, they may ask you to do something.

- Make sure you listen carefully and follow their instructions exactly. If you do not understand, ask them to tell you again.

- The emergency service you have asked for will soon be on its way to help you.

▲ *Remember to stay calm if you make an emergency call and give the operator as much information as you can.*

Glossary

addicted become so used to something that you cannot do without it.

antiseptic lotion, cream, liquid or spray that kills germs.

childproof something designed so that a child cannot operate it.

corrosive a substance that will eat into the skin and other materials.

current strong pull by water in one direction.

fluorescent giving off light.

germ a tiny thing that can cause illness.

gunpowder the mixture of chemicals that makes fireworks explode.

heatproof does not let heat through and is not damaged by heat.

illuminated lit up so that it is easy to see.

inflatable can be blown up by air, like a balloon.

panniers a pair of bags which are fixed on either side of a bicycle.

pedestrian a person who is walking.

precaution something done to prevent an accident happening.

reflective shines when a light shines on it.

waterproof does not let water through and is not damaged by water.

Other books to read

SAS Survival Skills by The Diagram Group
(Brockhampton Press, 1998)

The Extreme Survival Guide by Rory Storm
(Element Books Ltd, 2000)

Useful addresses

For more information on accidents and how to avoid
them contact:

The Royal Society for the Prevention of Accidents - RoSPA

help@rospa.co.uk

For more information on First Aid contact:

British Red Cross

9 Grosvenor Cresent

London

SW1X 7EJ

Tel: 020 7235 5454

information@redcross.org.uk

St. John's Ambulance

National Headquarters

27 St. John's Lane

London

EC1M 4BU

Tel: 08700 10 49 50

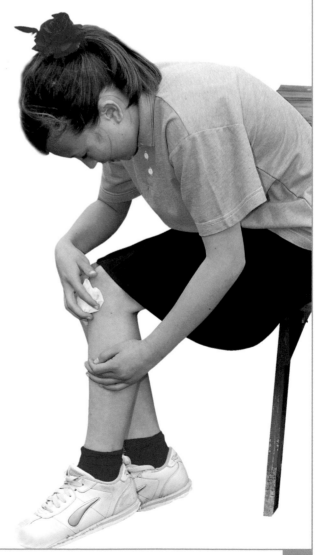

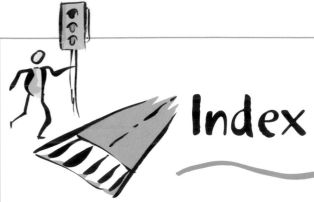

Index

All page numbers in **bold** refer to pictures as well as text